Sum of

This is the Day
Tim Tebow

Conversation Starters

By Paul Adams
Book Habits

Please Note: This is an unofficial Conversation Starters guide. If you have not yet read the original work, you can purchase the original book here.

Copyright © 2018 by BookHabits. All Rights Reserved. First Published in the United States of America 2018

We hope you enjoy this complimentary guide from BookHabits. Our mission is to aid readers and reading groups with quality thought-provoking material to in the discovery and discussions on some of today's favorite books.

Disclaimer / Terms of Use: This guide is unofficial and unauthorized. It is not authorized, approved, licensed, or endorsed by the original book's author or publisher and any of their licensees or affiliates. Product names, logos, brands, and other trademarks featured or referred to within this publication are the property of their respective trademark holders and are not affiliated with BookHabits. The publisher and author make no representations or warranties with respect to the accuracy or completeness of these contents and disclaim all warranties such as warranties of fitness for a particular purpose.

No part of this publication may be reproduced or retransmitted, electronic or mechanical, without the written permission of the publisher.

Bonus Downloads
*Get Free Books with **Any Purchase** of Conversation Starters!*

Every purchase comes with a FREE download!

Add spice to any conversation
Never run out of things to say
Spend time with those you love

Get it Now

or Click Here.

Scan Your Phone

Tips for Using Conversation Starters:

EVERY GOOD BOOK CONTAINS A WORLD FAR DEEPER THAN the surface of its pages. Questions herein are designed to bring us beneath the surface of the page and invite us into the world that lives on. These questions can be used to:

- Foster a deeper understanding of the book
- Promote an atmosphere of discussion for groups
- Assist in the study of the book, either individually or corporately
- Explore unseen realms of the book as never seen before

Table of Contents

Introducing *This is the Day* 6
Discussion Questions 14
Introducing the Author 35
Fireside Questions 42
Quiz Questions 53
Quiz Answers 66
Ways to Continue Your Reading 67

Introducing *This is the Day*

This is the Day: Reclaim Your Dream, Ignite Your Passion, Live Your Purpose is a book written by Tim Tebow (with A.J. Gregory). It is an inspirational book that encourages readers to live each day with a purpose. Tebow, an athlete and a Christian who has inspired his fans with his professional and spiritual example, shares how readers can lead inspiring lives as well.

Tebow says he wrote the book to help readers start to make changes in their lives. These changes do not have to be extraordinary leaps, nor something grand. They can be simple things but are important steps that can impact our lives. He mentions these small things can include believing in God's ways instead of doubting, doing instead of complaining or just paying attention to something or someone. He puts emphasis on what can be done today and in the moment. He tells readers that each day is an opportunity to change, to improve oneself, to create an impact on somebody else's life, to have a better view of a particular situation, or to create something meaningful. Time and age are not good reasons to put off doing things today. The first chapter opens with a first-person account of an emergency happening inside the plane where Tebow is in. Someone is having some kind of attack. Despite suggestions to sit down, Tebow goes to where the commotion is and prays with two women who ask him to pray with them while the others are trying to revive the man on the floor. Tebow goes on to tell how one of the women he prayed with that day lost her husband, and how he witnessed her struggle to cope with her husband's last hours from the plane to the hospital. Personal stories like this catch the readers' attention and enables Tebow to get his message across, that of making each day a significant one.

Tebow shares a lot of personal stories that give readers an inside look into his life and spiritual influences, including his parents and family. The first few pages relate to how Tebow would wake up in the mornings with his parents' songs. His mom would open the bedroom door singing the song

"This is the day that the Lord has made," while his father would sing "I'm alive, alert, awake, enthusiastic."

He begins each of the chapters with the first part of the title saying "This is the Day…" and ends them with action plan instructions such as Say I Love You, Leave the Past Behind, Get in the Game, and Listen to the Right Voice. The chapters end with a section entitled "Make This Your Day." The section provides questions that make readers think about how they lived the day. He provides wisdom nuggets that could easily be remembered. These include: "Without a powerful view of God and knowing what's possible through Him, our capacity to thrive is completely diminished; when you choose to live based on what God says and not what others say, you can live with confidence; He has a plan for you, and He has a purpose for your life. You can trust God's voice."

In the first chapter which has the title "This is the Day to Say 'I Love You'" Tebow includes a quotation from Victor Hugo which says " What a grand thing it is to be loved! What a far grander thing it is to love!" Tebow's writing style is described as readable and personable. His personal stories include not only his victories but his defeats and failures as well.

The book has 12 chapters, each emphasizing a particular lesson to learn. His stories cite examples of people who go through challenging situations and difficulties. His emphasis on faith in God is a strong element in the stories. Many of his stories include developments in his athletic career. Sports fans will learn that his decision to play baseball is a result of his being refused by football teams to get him as their quarterback. He now plays for the New York Mets. It is apparent in the book that Tebow's faith comes foremost in his life even while his love for football and baseball are also evident.

Amazon readers credit Tebow for putting his Christian values into action. They remember him as the football player who kneeled down to thank God every after a game. They like his message of not putting off for tomorrow the things that can be achieved starting today, including one's lifelong dreams, or fight one's addictions, or going against other personal challenges. He stresses the importance of creating meaning for one's life.

Nick Saban, a football coach and a personal friend of Tebow's says the book gives readers tools to achieve their dreams. He admires Tebow's philosophy in life as well as in his games. He accordingly speaks from real experience. NASCAR Championship winner Richard Petty says "Tim Tebow is all about living your dreams, but in a way that's meaningful—not just to become rich or famous or to look or feel good." He adds that the book teaches one how to become the person God has intended you to be. Actor Jamie Foxx says the book speaks to everyone no matter what one's gender, age, and economic status is. He stresses Tebow's advice to "find practical ways to start living a life that means something instead of letting life keep you down." Franklin Graham, head of Samaritan's Purse, says Tebow is strong and unswerving in his faith and is an inspiration to many. His new book will continue to inspire others.

This is the Day is a *New York Times* bestseller. Tebow is also the author of the *Times* bestseller *Through My Eyes*. He is the 2007 winner of the Heisman Trophy.

Discussion Questions

"Get Ready to Enter a New World"

Tip: Begin with questions dealing with broader issues to ensure ample time for quality discussions. Read through all discussion questions before engaging.

~~~

question 1

Tebow wrote the book to help readers start making changes in their lives. These changes do not have to be extraordinary leaps, nor something grand. They can be simple things but are important steps that can impact our lives. He mentions these small things can include believing in God's ways instead of doubting, doing instead of complaining or just paying attention to something or someone. Have you thought of making any changes in your life? Can you share what this is and why?

~~~

~~~

question 2

He puts emphasis on what can be done today and in the moment. He tells readers that each day is an opportunity to change, to improve oneself, to create an impact on somebody else's life, to have a better view of a particular situation, or to create something meaningful. Time and age are not good reasons to put off doing things today. Why is it important to start today and at the moment? What prevents you from making changes now?

~~~

question 3

The first chapter opens with a first-person account of an emergency happening inside the plane where Tebow is in. Someone is having some kind of attack. Despite suggestions to sit down, Tebow goes to where the commotion is and prays with two women who ask him to pray with them while the others are trying to revive the man on the floor. What eventually happens in this incident? Why does Tebow relate this incident?

~~~

~~~

question 4

Tebow shares a lot of personal stories that give readers an inside look into his life and spiritual influences, including his parents and family. Can the book be called a memoir? What do you learn about Tebow that you haven't known before?

~~~

~~~

question 5

The first few pages relate to how Tebow would wake up in the mornings with his parents' songs. His mom would open the bedroom door singing the song "This is the day that the Lord has made," while his father would sing "I'm alive, alert, awake, enthusiastic." What is the effect on Tebow waking up in the mornings like this? Would you like your parents to wake you up like this?

~~~

question 6

He begins each of the chapters with the first part of the title saying "This is the Day…" and ends them with action plan instructions such as Say I Love You, Leave the Past Behind, Get in the Game, and Listen to the Right Voice. What is the effect of reading the chapters like these? Do the chapters interest you?

~~~

question 7

The chapters end with a section entitled "Make This Your Day." The section provides questions that make readers think about how they lived the day. Do you like this part of the book? What is effect do these sections have on you?

~~~

~~~

question 8

He provides wisdom nuggets that could easily be remembered. These include: "Without a powerful view of God and knowing what's possible through Him, our capacity to thrive is completely diminished; when you choose to live based on what God says and not what others say, you can live with confidence; He has a plan for you, and He has a purpose for your life. You can trust God's voice." Which wisdom nugget do you particularly like? Why?

~~~

~~~

question 9

In the first chapter which says "This is the Day to Say 'I Love You'" Tebow includes a quotation from Victor Hugo which says " What a grand thing it is to be loved! What a far grander thing it is to love!" Who is Victor Hugo? Why does Tebow choose to quote him in this chapter?

~~~

~~~

question 10

Tebow's writing style is described as readable and personable. Do you find it easy to read the book? How would you describe Tebow's voice? What is it's effect on you?

~~~

~~~

question 11

His personal stories include not only his victories but his defeats and failures as well. Why does he include stories of his defeats and failures? How does he face his defeats and shortcomings?

~~~

question 12

The book has 12 chapters, each emphasizing a particular lesson to learn. His stories cite examples of people who go through challenging situations and difficulties. Which stories of other people did you find interesting? In what context does Tebow tell their stories?

~~~

question 13

His emphasis on faith in God is a strong element in the stories. How important is faith in God to Tebow? How important is it to you?

~~~

~~~

question 14

Many of his stories include developments in his athletic career. Sports fans will learn that his decision to play baseball is a result of his being refused by football teams to get him as their quarterback. He now plays for the New York Mets. Do his stories about his athletic career interest you? What successes in his career do you find interesting? How do these relate to his defeats?

~~~

question 15

It is apparent in the book that Tebow's faith comes foremost in his life even while his love for football and baseball are also evident. How does his identity as a Christian influence his athletic career? Does he make a separation between the two?

~~~

question 16

Amazon readers credit Tebow for putting his Christian values into action. They remember him as the football player who kneeled down to thank God every after a game. They like his message of not putting off for tomorrow the things that can be achieved starting today, including one's lifelong dreams, or fight one's addictions, or going against other personal challenges. He stresses the importance of creating meaning for one's life. What characteristic of Tebow's inspires you? Why?

~~~

~~~

question 17

Nick Saban, a football coach and a personal friend of Tebow's says the book gives readers tools to achieve their dreams. He admires Tebow's philosophy in life as well as in his games. He accordingly speaks from real experience. Without considering his Christian faith, how does Tebow's athletic profession make him a better person?

~~~

~~~

question 18

NASCAR Championship winner Richard Petty says "Tim Tebow is all about living your dreams, but in a way that's meaningful—not just to become rich or famous or to look or feel good." He adds that the book teaches one how to become the person God has intended you to be. Do you think God intends everybody to be successful like Tebow? Is succeeding part of God's plan for you?

~~~

question 19

Actor Jamie Foxx says the book speaks to everyone no matter what one's gender, age, and economic status is. He stresses Tebow's advice to "find practical ways to start living a life that means something instead of letting life keep you down." Do you think Tebow's book speaks to non-athletes, women, and people of color, as well? If yes, why do you think he speaks to a wide audience?

~~~

~~~

question 20

This is the Day is a New York Times bestseller. His first book, Through My Eyes, is also a Times bestseller. His second book, Shaken, is, however, not a bestseller. Why do you think it was not as popular as his two other books?

~~~

Introducing the Author

Timothy Richard Tebow played professional football before turning to his current profession as baseball outfielder for the New York Mets organization. He was the winner of the Heisman Trophy in 2007 as a college football player for the University of Florida. He joined the Denver Broncos in the 2010 NFL Draft and played with them for two seasons. Afterward, he joined the New York Jets, The New England Patriots, and the Philadelphia Eagles in 2012, 2013, and 2015, respectively. He last played for the Philadelphia Eagles in 2015. Released by the Eagles in September of that same year, he has not been invited by any other team afterward.

Tebow is noted in NFL history as the only quarterback who has not reached 30 years old and who has won a playoff game and then not hired again by any football team, forcing him to retire early.

In 2016, he started his career as a professional baseball player, signing a contract with the New York Mets, which revived his athletic career.

Tebow was born in Manila, Philippines on August 14, 1987, by his missionary parents. His family moved to Jacksonville, Florida when he was three years old. He was homeschooled by his parents and was able to play high school football for Allen D. Nease High School. He became known for his outstanding football performance in high school and was twice awarded the Player of the Year and was also named Mr. Football in his senior year for leading the Nease Panthers to state championship. ESPN featured him in the documentary "Faces in Sports," citing him for his unique position as a homeschooled students who played for a traditional high school. His missionary work in the Philippines was also featured. He attended the University of Florida on an athletic scholarship, playing for the Florida Gators and coach Urban Meyer who Tebow particularly cited as a reason why he chose to join the Gators. He won the

Heisman Trophy in 2007 while playing for the team and was thrice awarded the Most Valuable Player of the year.

Tebow's first book is entitled *Through My Eyes* co-authored with Nathan Whitaker. It was published in 2011. The book is autobiographical, detailing his growing up years till he reached college. It includes his experiences as a college football player. The book became a *New York Times bestseller* in 2012, staying in the bestseller list for 24 weeks. It was the top bestselling sports book and top bestselling religious book in 2011. He wrote an edition for young readers. His second book, *Shaken: Discovering Your True Identity in the Midst of Life's Storms* was published in 2016. It talks about Tebow's experience as a promising athlete whose career reached its heights when he joined the Florida Gators and then the Denver Broncos but was eventually traded to the New York Jets, after which he was let go after one season. *Shaken* talks about how his self-identity was put into question and how he found his grounding and real identity in God. The book is awarded the Christian Book of the Year for 2017. Tebow is known for his missionary work in the Philippines. He has visited schools and villages around the country, preaching his Christian faith and supporting evangelical organizations. He is one of the leaders of the Fellowship of Christian Athletes which advocates sexual purity, a Christian belief that dissuades sex outside marriage and homosexual acts. The neologism "tebowing" is coined after Tebow's habit of kneeling down and praying which he always does after his team's victorious games. The NFL issued a rule in 2010 banning players from using eye black to paint messages. The rule was also called the Tebow Rule. Tebow used to write biblical verses with his eye black, making the messages popular among football and non-football fans.

Bonus Downloads
Get Free Books with **Any Purchase** *of* Conversation Starters!

Every purchase comes with a FREE download!

Add spice to any conversation
Never run out of things to say
Spend time with those you love

Get it Now

or Click Here.

Scan Your Phone

Fireside Questions

"What would you do?"

Tip: These questions can be a fun exercise as it spurs creativity among the readers by allowing alternate scene endings and "if this was you" questions.

~~~

question 21

He joined the Denver Broncos in the 2010 NFL Draft and played with them for two seasons. Afterward, he joined the New York Jets, The New England Patriots, and the Philadelphia Eagles in 2012, 2013, and 2015, respectively. He last played for the Philadelphia Eagles in 2015. Released by the Eagles in September of that same year, he has not been invited by any other team afterward. Tebow is noted in NFL history as the only quarterback who has not reached 30 years old and who has won a playoff game and then not hired again by any football team, forcing him to retire early. Why did his football career suddenly come to a halt? Could he have done something else to revive it?

~~~

~~~

question 22

In 2016, he started his career as a professional baseball player, signing a contract with the New York Mets, which revived his athletic career. How does he describe his shift to baseball? How does he see it in terms of God's purpose for him?

~~~

~~~

question 23

Tebow was born in Manila, Philippines on August 14, 1987, by his missionary parents. His family moved to Jacksonville, Florida when he was three years old. He was homeschooled by his parents and was able to play high school football for Allen D. Nease High School. How was his high school football performance? What awards did he win?

~~~

~~~

question 24

His second book, Shaken: Discovering Your True Identity in the Midst of Life's Storms was published in 2016. It talks about Tebow's experience as a promising athlete whose career reached its heights when he joined the Florida Gators and then the Denver Broncos. But he was eventually traded to the New York Jets, after which he was let go after one season. How does he explain his self-identity in the book? What feelings and fears did he experience and how did he overcome them?

~~~

question 25

The NFL issued a rule in 2010 banning players from using eye black to paint messages. The rule was also called the Tebow Rule. Tebow used to write biblical verses with his eye black, making the messages popular among football and non-football fans. What biblical verses did he write with his eye black? How popular was it among fans?

~~~

~~~

question 26

This is the Day is an inspirational book that encourages readers to live each day with a purpose. Tebow, an athlete and a Christian who has inspired his fans with his professional and spiritual example, shares how readers can lead inspiring lives as well. If you are not a Christian, do you think you can still learn something from this book? Why? Why not?

~~~

~~~

question 27

He begins each of the chapters with the first part of the title saying "This is the Day…" and ends them with action plan instructions such as Say I Love You, Leave the Past Behind, Get in the Game, and Listen to the Right Voice. If you are to add another chapter to the book, what would it be about? Why?

~~~

~~~

question 28

His personal stories include not only his victories but his defeats and failures as well. If he did not include stories about his defeats, how would the book be like? Would it be as interesting? Why? Why not?

~~~

~~~

question 29

His stories cite examples of people who go through challenging situations and difficulties. If he focused all his stories about other people instead of stories about his life, would the book be a good one? Why? Why not?

~~~

question 30

Actor Jamie Foxx says the book speaks to everyone no matter what one's gender, age, and economic status is. If the book limited its readership to athletes and sports fans, do you think it would be a bestseller? What would be the advantage of focusing on a certain kind of audience?

~~~

Quiz Questions

"Ready to Announce the Winners?"

Tip: Create a leaderboard and track scores to see who gets the most correct answers. Winners required. Prizes optional.

~~~

quiz question 1

The first few pages relate to how Tebow would wake up in the mornings with his parents' songs. His mom would open the bedroom door singing the song _____.

~~~

~~~

quiz question 2

The chapters end with a section entitled _____. The section provides questions that make readers think about how they lived the day.

~~~

~~~

quiz question 3

In the first chapter which says "This is the Day to Say 'I Love You'" Tebow includes a quotation from _____ which says " What a grand thing it is to be loved! What a far grander thing it is to love!"

~~~

~~~

quiz question 4

True or False: The book has 12 chapters, each emphasizing a particular lesson to learn.

~~~

~~~

quiz question 5

True or False: His emphasis on faith in God is a strong element in the stories.

~~~

~~~

quiz question 6

True or False: He begins each of the chapters with the first part of the title saying "This is the Day…" and ends them with action plan instructions such as Say I Love You, Leave the Past Behind, Get in the Game, and Listen to the Right Voice.

~~~

~~~

quiz question 7

True or False: Many of his stories include developments in his love life.

~~~

~~~

quiz question 8

Timothy Richard Tebow played professional football before turning to his current profession as _____ outfielder for the New York Mets organization.

~~~

~ ~ ~

quiz question 9

He joined the _____ in the 2010 NFL Draft and played with them for two seasons.

~ ~ ~

~~~

quiz question 10

True or False: In 2016, he started his career as a professional baseball player, signing a contract with the New York Mets, which revived his athletic career.

~~~

~~~

quiz question 11

True or False: Tebow was born in Nigeria on August 14, 1987, by his missionary parents.

~~~

~~~

quiz question 12

True or False: He won the Heisman Trophy in 2007 while playing for the Florida Gators and was thrice awarded the Most Valuable Player of the year.

~~~

Quiz Answers

1. This is the day that the Lord has made
2. Make This Your Day."
3. Victor Hugo
4. True
5. True
6. True
7. False
8. baseball
9. Denver Broncos
10. True
11. False
12. True

Ways to Continue Your Reading

EVERY month, our team runs through a wide selection of books to pick the best titles for readers and reading groups, and promotes these titles to our thousands of readers – sometimes with free downloads, sale dates, and additional brochures.

Click here to sign up for these benefits.

If you have not yet read the original work or would like to read it again, you can purchase the original book here.

Bonus Downloads
*Get Free Books with **Any Purchase** of Conversation Starters!*

Every purchase comes with a FREE download!

Add spice to any conversation
Never run out of things to say
Spend time with those you love

Get it Now

or Click Here.

Scan Your Phone

On the Next Page...

If you found this book helpful to your discussions and rate it a 4 or 5, please write us a review on the next page.

Any length would be fine but we'd appreciate hearing you more! We'd be very encouraged.

Till next time,

BookHabits

"*Loving Books is Actually a Habit*"

CPSIA information can be obtained
at www.ICGtesting.com
Printed in the USA
BVHW032242200319
543304BV00001B/35/P